UNPLUG

BREATHE

CREATE

I0418260

A MONTH OF FINDING CREATIVITY IN CHAOS THROUGH MEDITATION

Unplug Breathe Create: A Month of Finding Creativity In Chaos Through Meditation is a work of my own creation.

The information in this book was correct at the time of publication, and the Author does not assume any liability for loss or damage caused by errors or omissions, again, this is my perspective, opinion, and experience, so it has been written as such.

ISBN - 979-8-9875738-5-3

Cover, Book Design, and Layout by megs thompson, megswrites llc
www.megswrites.com

www.inomniaparatuspublishing.com

"CHAOS IS THE FIRST STEP IN THE CREATIVE PROCESS."

—DR. JILL BOLTE TAYLOR

This journal is part of the UNPLUG BREATHE CREATE series & designed to be used alongside a bespoke guided meditation.

Download this month's meditation using the QR code below:

HOW TO BEST USE THIS JOURNAL & MEDITATION

UNPLUG

The first step to reconnecting with ourselves as creative beings is to unplug & disconnect even temporarily from the countless electronic tethers that keep us firmly held in the world of shoulds & must's.

BREATHE

Take a few deep breaths, paying close attention to the way oxygen moves through your mouth & nose, filling your lungs & reawakening the creative genius locked safely within you, exhaling any fears, hesitations, or doubts that may filter your magic.

CREATE

Release your desire to control, plan & perfect every step & movement you make. Embrace the often wild, messy & chaotic magic that comes with allowing your inner creative to explore & play. Prepare yourself to experience fulfillment & satisfaction in new & creative ways.

DAILY ROUTINE

While moving through your day, begin implementing the use of affirmations. Both habits & beliefs are formed & strengthened through consistent repetition & before you know it your thoughts will become truths.

Included below are powerful affirmations that when paired with your daily tasks & activities, will empower you through this month of finding & claiming your own creative space.

I recommend repeating one or more of these affirmations aloud anytime you find yourself in front of a mirror, washing your hands, or refilling your beverage of choice.

I AM COMFORTABLE IN CHAOS

I AM CONSTANTLY CREATING

I AM DOING EXACTLY WHAT I'M MEANT TO BE DOING, AT EXACTLY THE RIGHT TIME

30-DAY ENERGY TRACKER

When you've completed your daily meditation, make note of a single word or phrase that best describes your energy level in that moment.

Day 1	Day 2	Day 3	Day 4	Day 5
Day 6	Day 7	Day 8	Day 9	Day 10
Day 11	Day 12	Day 13	Day 14	Day 15
Day 16	Day 17	Day 18	Day 19	Day 20
Day 21	Day 22	Day 23	Day 24	Day 25
Day 26	Day 27	Day 28	Day 29	Day 30

DAY 1

In a world where conformity & efficiency routinely drown out creativity & originality, it's of extreme importance that we schedule specific times within our days & weeks to lean into our more creative side. How do you feel about the idea of planning your creative time? Is there a specific time of day when you feel most creative? Spend a few moments journaling on these thoughts, as well as creating appointments for yourself in your planner or calendar, for your 'creative dates with yourself'

ON A SCALE OF 1-5 WHAT'S YOUR
CURRENT CREATIVITY LEVEL?

DAY 2

How many times have you started a new creative project, only to lose interest & allow it to gather dust on the shelf? It's important that we finish the things we've started. This seemingly simply act develops a sense of discipline within ourselves.

ON A SCALE OF 1-5 WHAT'S YOUR
CURRENT CREATIVITY LEVEL?

DAY 3

It may feel counterintuitive when the world is twisting & turning in different & unexpected ways, but slowing down is what gives the space & oxygen for creativity to manifest. Where in your daily life can you slow down & allow for creativity to manifest?

ON A SCALE OF 1-5 WHAT'S YOUR
CURRENT CREATIVITY LEVEL?

DAY 4

To fully embrace your creative spirit, we need a well-rested mind & quiet space to connect with our inner voice & inspiration. How do you currently provide yourself with that self-care & rest? How might you better take care of yourself?

ON A SCALE OF 1-5 WHAT'S YOUR
CURRENT CREATIVITY LEVEL?

DAY 5

Inspiration from our environment cannot be overestimated. There's a reason many of us experience our best ideas in the shower, while walking in a garden, or driving the car. By stepping away from our routine & day-to-day workspace & allowing our surroundings to draw out & flex our that creative muscle. How are you currently stepping away? How might you be able to do this more often?

ON A SCALE OF 1-5 WHAT'S YOUR
CURRENT CREATIVITY LEVEL?

DAY 6

Often, we fear the idea of 'getting messy,' & allow this to keep us from following our creative spirit. How are you allowing & encouraging yourself to get messy & enjoy the creative process?

ON A SCALE OF 1-5 WHAT'S YOUR
CURRENT CREATIVITY LEVEL?

DAY 7

Believe it or not, chaos is our friend. Chaos invites us to generate new ideas, to explore new pathways & to find creative solutions to issues & situations. Reflect on the past week, how has chaos encouraged you to think outside of the box?

ON A SCALE OF 1-5 WHAT'S YOUR
CURRENT CREATIVITY LEVEL?

DAY 8

Dr. Robert Bilder, a psychiatry & psychology professor at UCLA's Semel Institute for Neuroscience and Human Behavior, once said, "The truly creative changes & the big shifts occur right at the edge of chaos." Where in your life have you experienced chaos leading to big shifts & changes?

ON A SCALE OF 1-5 WHAT'S YOUR
CURRENT CREATIVITY LEVEL?

DAY 9

Attitude is half the battle in chaotic situations. How do you currently own your attitude? How might you be able to better choose your attitude? For many, this can be something as simple as smiling more.

ON A SCALE OF 1-5 WHAT'S YOUR
CURRENT CREATIVITY LEVEL?

DAY 10

Sometimes in life things seem random, as if they have no purpose, meaning or shape. However, when we step back & take a look at the bigger picture, patterns form & the seeming chaos we've been experiencing, suddenly makes perfect sense. Where in life have you been experiencing chaos? Take a step back & focus on the bigger picture. Does the bigger picture provide clarity for your experiences?

ON A SCALE OF 1-5 WHAT'S YOUR
CURRENT CREATIVITY LEVEL?

DAY 11

On a scale of 1-10, how strongly do you trust yourself in times of chaos? What contributed to this rating? How do you feel you might be able to better strengthen that trust in yourself?

_____

_____

_____

_____

_____

_____

_____

_____

_____

_____

_____

_____

_____

_____

ON A SCALE OF 1-5 WHAT'S YOUR
CURRENT CREATIVITY LEVEL?

DAY 12

Often, chaos can seem overwhelming, because we're looking at an entire jumbled puzzle, all at once. However, when we're able to focus on only one or two pieces at a time, we can better address those pieces, before moving onto others. A great way of doing this is to delegate responsibility for some pieces to others. In the space below create a list of the tasks in your daily/weekly/monthly life that can be delegated.

_____

_____

_____

_____

_____

_____

_____

_____

_____

_____

_____

ON A SCALE OF 1-5 WHAT'S YOUR
CURRENT CREATIVITY LEVEL?

DAY 13

Reflecting on the list you made yesterday, choose one task that you can delegate to someone else this week? This may be in your personal or professional life. Who can you delegate that task to?

ON A SCALE OF 1-5 WHAT'S YOUR
CURRENT CREATIVITY LEVEL?

DAY 14

Reflecting back on your musings from yesterday.
What hesitations do you feel around asking for
support? When you do delegate tasks to others, are
you able to let go of your attachment to the task, or
do you continue to find it taking up space in your
mind?

ON A SCALE OF 1-5 WHAT'S YOUR
CURRENT CREATIVITY LEVEL?

DAY 15

How did you most enjoy expressing yourself
creatively as a child, before you began experiencing
the chaos that comes with being an adult? Is that
something you might still enjoy today?

ON A SCALE OF 1-5 WHAT'S YOUR
CURRENT CREATIVITY LEVEL?

DAY 16

When was the last time you created something for
fun, without purpose or direction? How confident
did you feel? What did you enjoy most about the
process? What hesitations did you experience? Were
you able to fully ignore the chaos around you?

ON A SCALE OF 1-5 WHAT'S YOUR
CURRENT CREATIVITY LEVEL?

DAY 17

What is it about the chaos in your life that keeps you feeling stressed, frustrated, overwhelmed, or lost? How are you able to soothe those feelings?

ON A SCALE OF 1-5 WHAT'S YOUR
CURRENT CREATIVITY LEVEL?

DAY 18

Stand in front of a mirror & while looking at your reflection, tell yourself that you are safe. You are powerful. Nothing horrible will befall you, if you choose to take a break, a walk, a nap, color a picture, write a short story, or give yourself a facial. Now, what are you going to do today, for you?

ON A SCALE OF 1-5 WHAT'S YOUR
CURRENT CREATIVITY LEVEL?

DAY 19

What is one task that you complete everyday. This may be something mundane, administrative & without much sparkle. How can you approach this task from a more creative standpoint?

ON A SCALE OF 1-5 WHAT'S YOUR
CURRENT CREATIVITY LEVEL?

DAY 20

How can you weave more creativity, confidence & joy into your daily life? Perhaps it's dancing while cleaning house, wearing silly socks, or replacing the words, 'I think' with 'I know,' for an entire day.

ON A SCALE OF 1-5 WHAT'S YOUR
CURRENT CREATIVITY LEVEL?

DAY 21

Failure is a part of life, it's also part of the creative process. When did you last fail during a creative project? Focus on the fact that while the outcome may have fallen short of your intention, it was temporary & there is no reason to not try again.

ON A SCALE OF 1-5 WHAT'S YOUR
CURRENT CREATIVITY LEVEL?

DAY 22

Through the meditation, you visualized your physical body, with numerous strings attached to different areas of chaos in your life. What were some of those areas or tasks? Have you been able to delegate any of these? Have you been able to address any of these by tapping into your creative side?

ON A SCALE OF 1-5 WHAT'S YOUR
CURRENT CREATIVITY LEVEL?

DAY 23

Spend a few moments reflecting on the things you're grateful for right now, in this moment. There's nothing too small or weird. Often we find ourselves lost in the chaos, and the first step to activating your own abundance is to recognize & appreciate the countless things you already possess.

ON A SCALE OF 1-5 WHAT'S YOUR
CURRENT CREATIVITY LEVEL?

DAY 24

What areas of your life contain excessive chaos that you can let go of in order to make room for opportunities & experiences? Why have you been holding onto these things? How have they been serving you? How have they been limiting you?

ON A SCALE OF 1-5 WHAT'S YOUR
CURRENT CREATIVITY LEVEL?

DAY 25

What does satisfaction look like to you? How does it feel? Where in your body do you feel satisfaction?

ON A SCALE OF 1-5 WHAT'S YOUR
CURRENT CREATIVITY LEVEL?

DAY 26

What are you big, hairy, scary goals for the next 6 months? Do you genuinely believe that these goals are attainable? What actions are you taking to manifest these goals? Have you fully committed to your own success?

ON A SCALE OF 1-5 WHAT'S YOUR
CURRENT CREATIVITY LEVEL?

DAY 27

Looking back at the big, hairy, scary goals you outlined yesterday, reframe those goals below as having already come to fruition. For example: In 6 months I want to have signed 5 new authentically aligned clients, becomes, Over the past 6 months I've connected with & signed creative agreements with 5 authentically aligned clients. How does it feel to reframe these goals as facts?

ON A SCALE OF 1-5 WHAT'S YOUR
CURRENT CREATIVITY LEVEL?

DAY 28

Think of 10 people in your life, these can be friends, family members, colleagues, or people that you admire. How do these individuals manage stress & chaos? Do you seem similarities in yourself? Or traits that you'd like to adopt yourself?

ON A SCALE OF 1-5 WHAT'S YOUR
CURRENT CREATIVITY LEVEL?

DAY 29

Where in your life do you feel chaos the most? Work, love, money, faith? What does chaos feel like for you? What does it look like?

ON A SCALE OF 1-5 WHAT'S YOUR
CURRENT CREATIVITY LEVEL?

DAY 30

How are you currently coping with chaos & how might you like to handle it differently in the future? The best time to change your attitude & feelings about chaos is now. Take back the control of your life, moving confidently & creatively in the direction of your dreams.

ON A SCALE OF 1-5 WHAT'S YOUR
CURRENT CREATIVITY LEVEL?

If you already have an UNPLUG BREATHE CREATE subscription, keep an eye on your mailbox for your next delivery.

If you aren't yet a member but would like to be, or are interested in gifting a membership to someone else, scan the QR code below.